The Church
Fanelda Westphalen
Photography By Dana Schroeder

"Here is the church;

and here is the steeple.

Open the door and
here are the people.

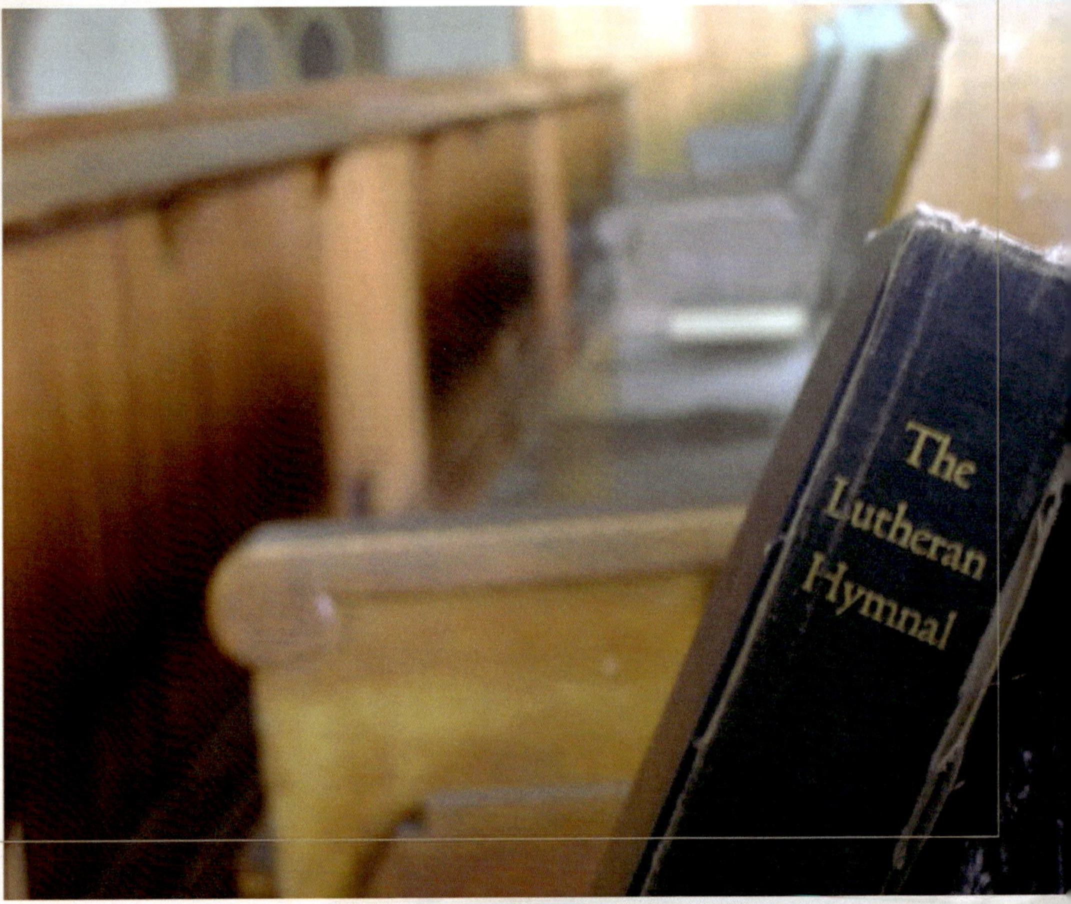

Close the door and the people pray.

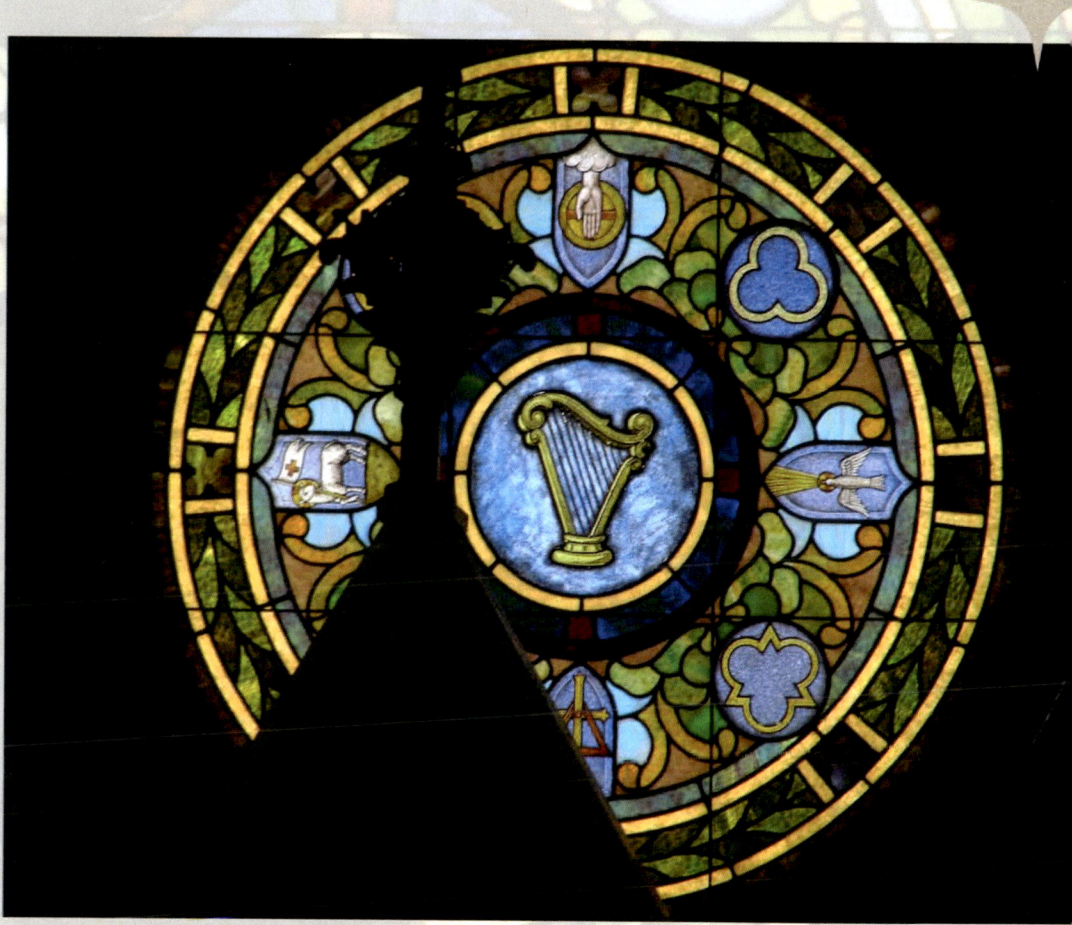

Open the door and they walk away."

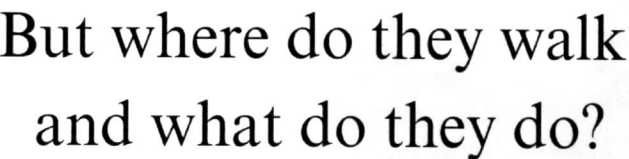

But where do they walk
and what do they do?

This is the question to answer honest and true!

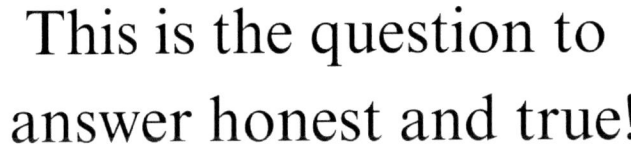

Each believer is the church at work on earth

Seeking to find and
use his God-given worth.

The success of the task is…

measured by being a willing tool

And allowing God the whole of our hearts to rule.

Our personality and skills are used in a unique way

To give glory to God…

and Him honor to pay.

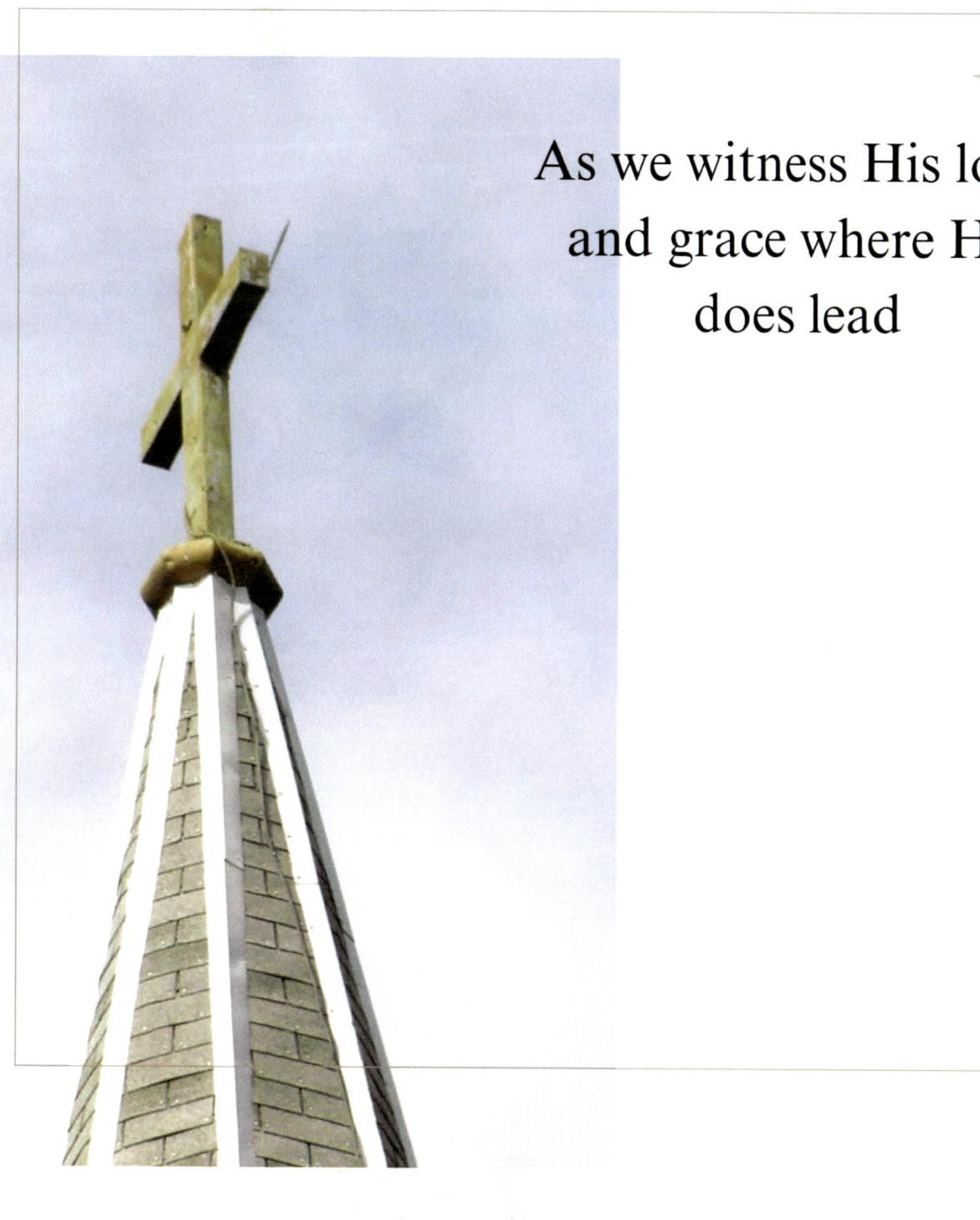

As we witness His love and grace where He does lead

We serve Him, as His children we willingly feed.

Whether physical or spiritual it matter not a bit,

For doing things for God causes an inner Light to be lit.

Ministering to the sick, imprisoned, hungry, or cold

Will help to win others as part of God's fold.

Giving a cup of cold water in His holy name

Cause giver and receiver to both have some of God's gain

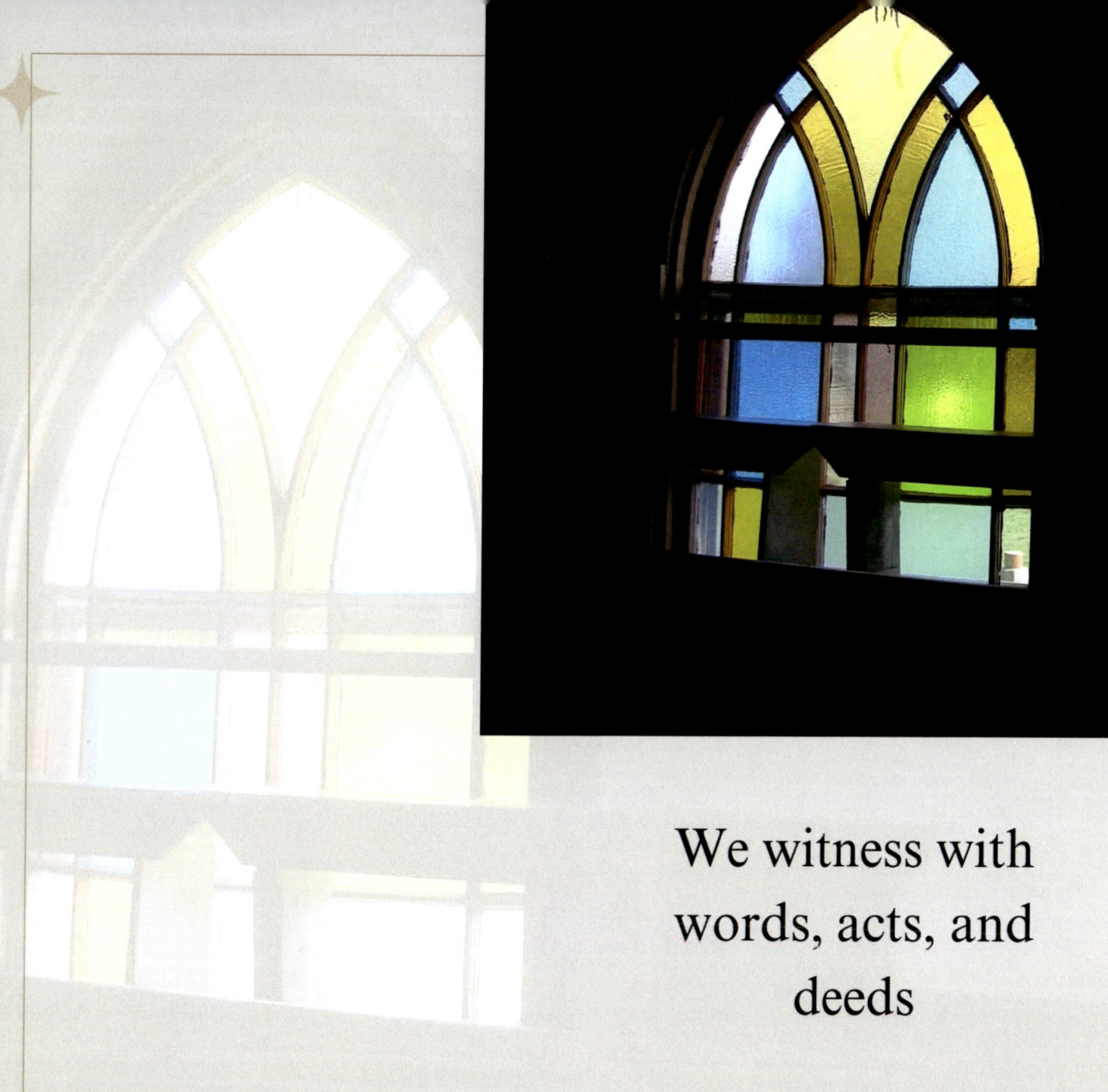

We witness with words, acts, and deeds

While trying
through
God to meet
His children's
needs

If it's writing a letter or reading to the blind,

Helping the homeless, sharing with the lonely a little time;

Praying for the sick, hurting, or those making decisions;

Sharing God's Word to those whose lives need revision—

Any charitable act given to another in God's holy name

Shows a touch of God's wonder to the spiritually lame.

Being God's hands and
feet at work on earth

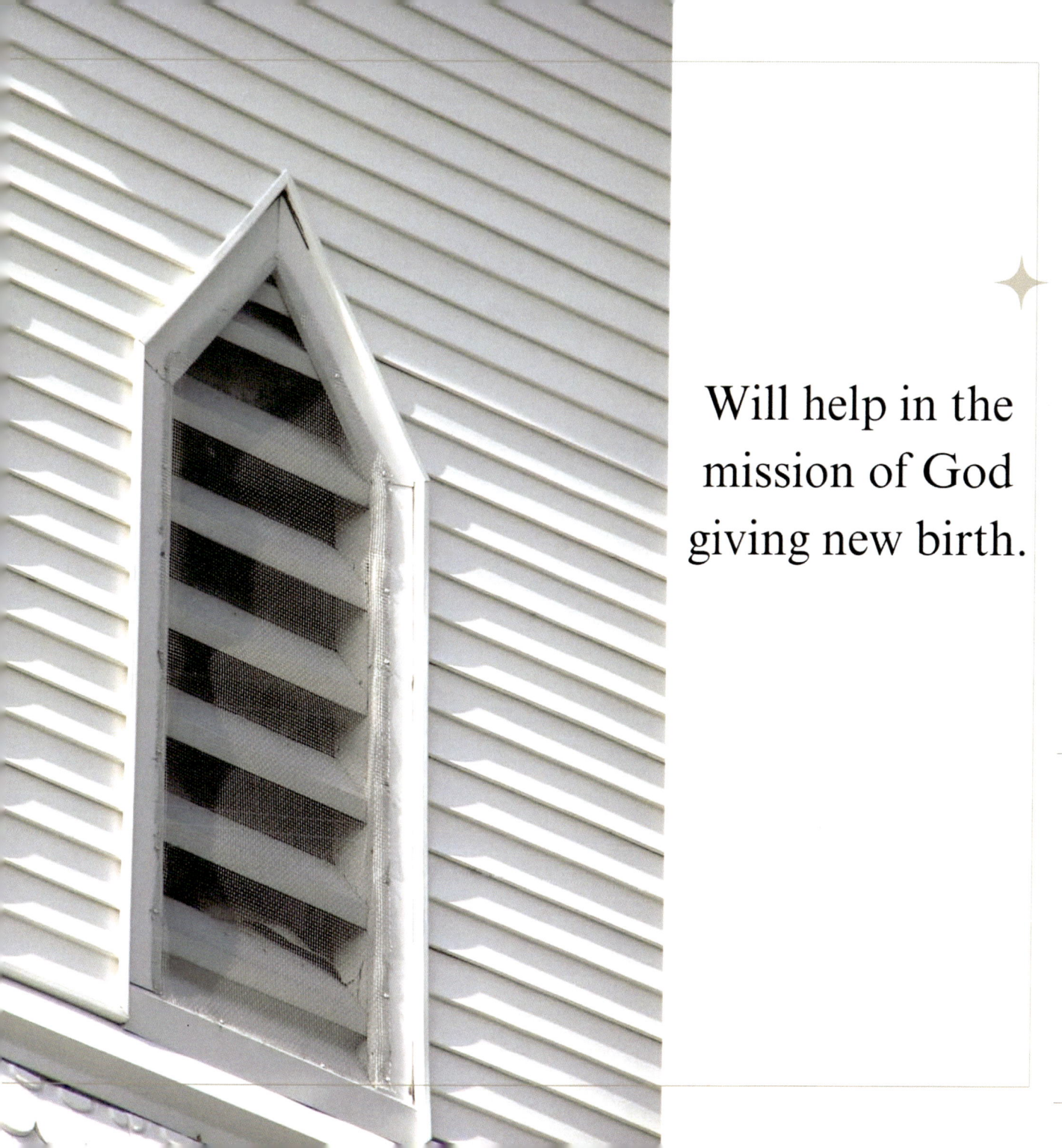

Will help in the mission of God giving new birth.

Are we as the church alive and well?

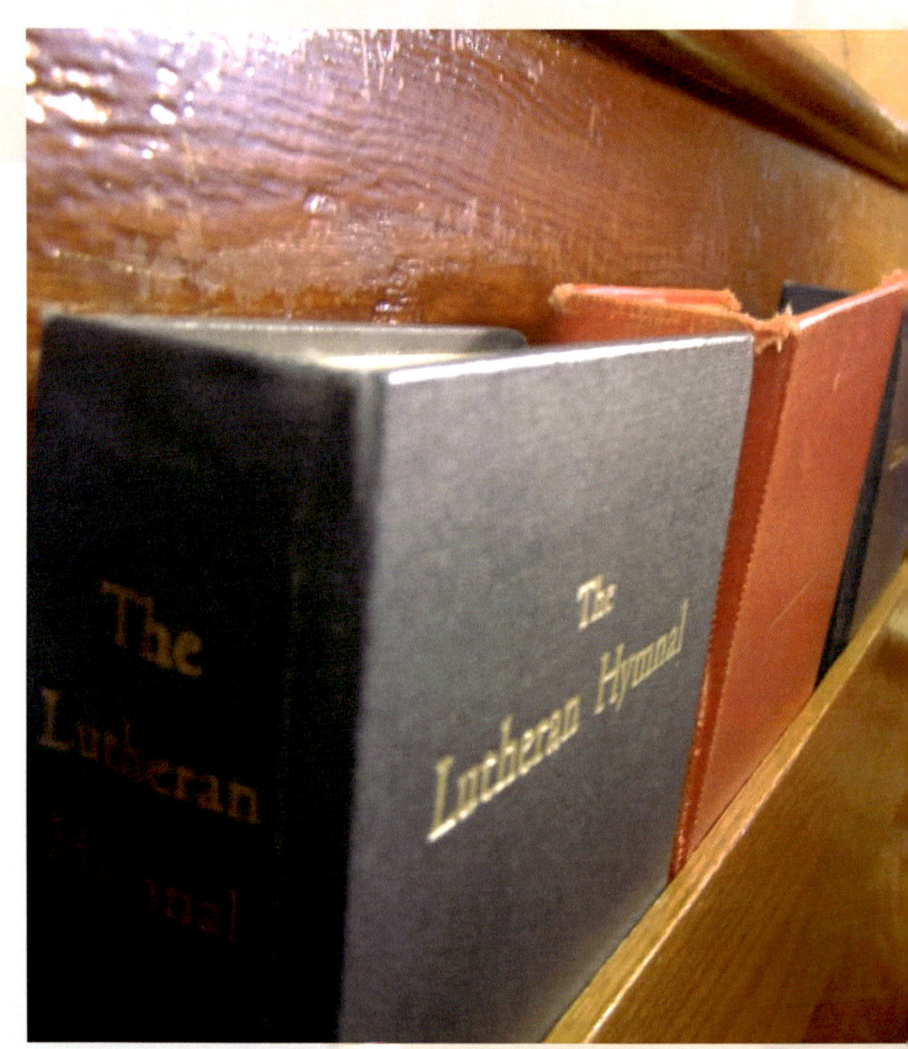

Are we doing our part to make the invisible church swell?

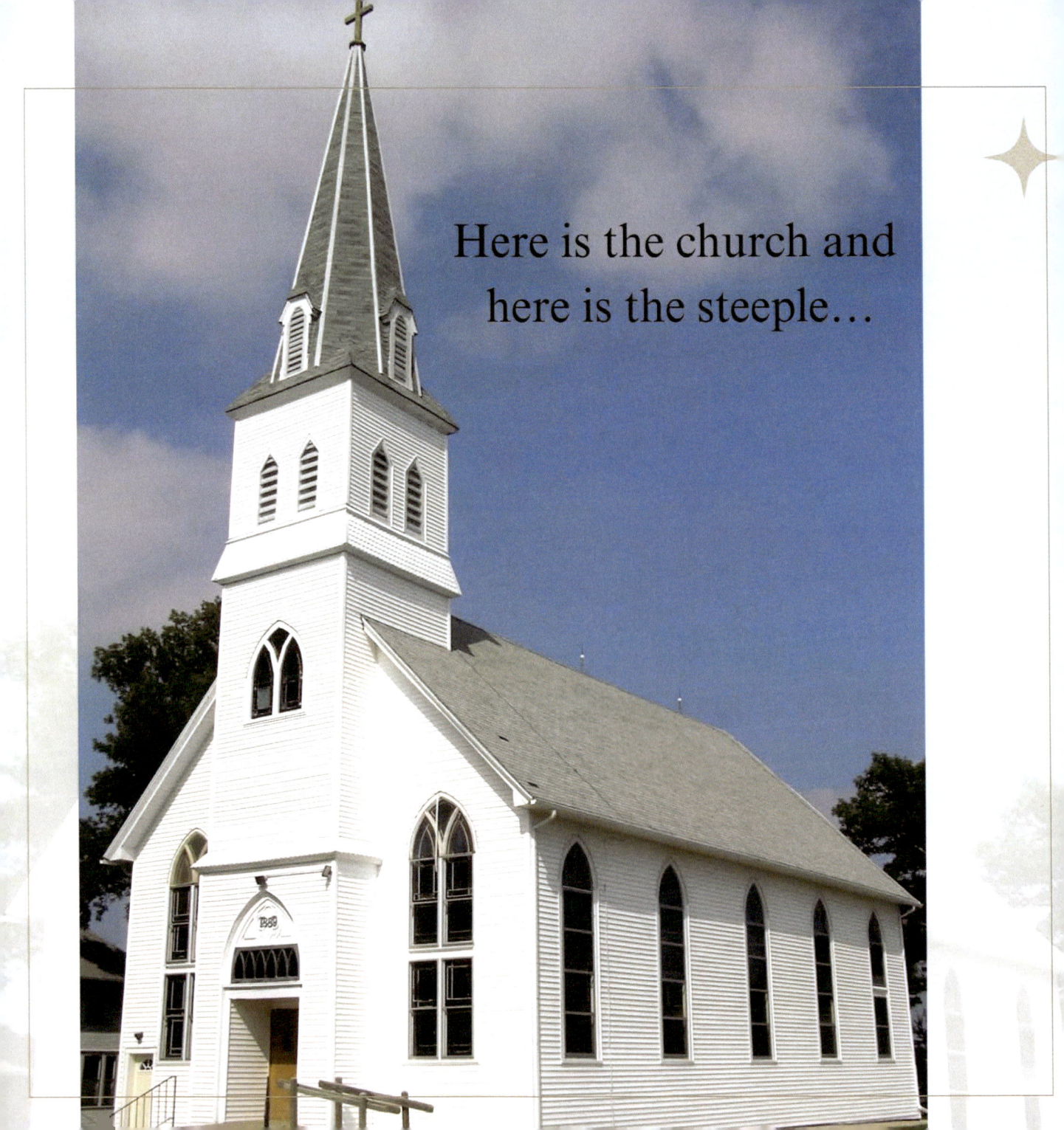

Are you at
work,
as one of God's
chosen people?

Copyright @ 2024 by Marla Schoening, Charla & Co, LLC • Photography @ 1998 by Dana Schroeder • Poetry Copyright @ 1998 by Fanelda Westphalen • Published in the United States by IngramSpark ingramspark.com and Charla & Co www.charlaandco.com • All rights reserved. In accordance with the US copyright act of 1976, the scanning, uploading, and electronic sharing of any part of this book without the permission of the publisher is unlawful piracy and theft of the authors intellectual property. If you would like to use material from the book, other than for review purposes, prior written permission must be obtained by contacting the publisher at marla@charlaaandco.com Thank you for your support of the author's rights. • Charla & Company LLC • Ingramspark • First Edition: July1998 • Names: Westphalen, Fanelda, author. Schroeder, Dana, photographer. • Title: The Church/Fanelda Westphalen • Identifiers: 979-8-9880011-0-2 (Hardback) • Subjects: Bibles | Architecture | Poetry • Hardcover ISBN: 979-8-9880011-0-2 • 2nd Edition, July 2024 • Printed in the United States of America